101

I Taught
My Son

by

Paul Lawrence

101 Lessons I Taught My Son

Inspirational Book of Quotations

Published by Lawrence Publishing

Printed in the United Kingdom

First Printing 2017 Lawrence Publishing.

ISBN 978-0-9957031-0-0

"Paul is not the first man of colour to raise a child, but he may be the first to so articulately and simply lay down a blueprint for some of the challenges we parents and our children face today.

I will definitely be using and adopting it for my two young boys. As Paúl says, everybody is different and therefore adaptation is a must. I am waiting for the part two. Dealing with mobile phones, girlfriends, intimacy. Who did he turn to when surely the diplomacy of a woman was needed? I can't wait.

In truth, these are guidelines. Roots. If we can get the foundations right, there are no limitations for what our children can achieve. It gives us confidence that when adversity strikes, they will be able to react with kindness and common sense.

I am sincerely hoping this book can be used in schools too because for many children, the teacher or mentor (in the case of the fabulous Urban Synergy) is the closest they will come to having a parent. Sad but true. Well done sir."

~Eddie Nestor
Actor, Compere and Host of Drivetime on BBC Radio London 94.9

"An absolute page turner! This book may well be lessons for Kaream, but, in actual fact, they are lessons for us all. Some great gems here, and great insight. I love this book! A must have!"

~Angie Le Mar
Comedienne/Writer

"Funny, familiar, poignant and profound – the 101 lessons in this book represent the kind of wisdom that we fathers hope we are smart enough to impart to our sons. An excellent and timeless collection!"

Kolarele Sonaike
President, 100 Black Men of London 2015–2017, Barrister, Father

Dedications

This book is dedicated to Tony, Carmel, Hubert and Kaream.

Contents

Foreword

Parenting breeds a natural sense of love and responsibility for all sentient beings, particularly humans. It carries with it the burden of expectation, the many years of cajoling, teaching and instruction, the moments of disappointment, tempered by those other moments of joy. Of course, ideas about parenting evolve over time, and at one level is culturally specific. It is both a challenge and opportunity and will no doubt impact on the consciousness of both parent and child.

In a global economy now characterized, particularly in the West, by low and underpaid employment for young people generally, but for young black men, in particular, it is understandable that a black father has sought to treat his parental responsibility with a defined focus and seriousness. Black fathers in this environment have been historically depicted, ignoring the inhumane impact of slavery, as feckless and irresponsible. Hence that urban myth that black youth criminality is a result of absent fathers and that it has nothing to do with a historically and racially defined label, *it is just the way they are*.

Paul Lawrence's short book, containing just fourteen short and easily digestible chapters seeks to debunk that stereotype. Yes, it is written by a black father with a direct and simple message to a black male child, yet its themes simply highlight many core values in the perennial parental quest to produce: well-adjusted, caring, aware, personally and socially responsible adults that speak beyond racial and class boundaries. It asks us: what does it mean to be a good parent? It questions whether there is a set of simple, yet universal propositions that, whilst not necessarily comprehensive, encapsulate core themes of parenting from which we can all learn, irrespective of race and class.

It eschews the deceit of the hologram of the perfect parent, for there is no perfect way of being a parent. Each child, we know, enters the world throbbing with its own unique personality and identity, which can be moulded but not dramatically changed. Recognising that, it cautions that to understand and nurture your child, you must first understand yourself as a parent in order to guard against bestowing upon your child the baggage of one's own emotional legacy.

It is personally pertinent for me, as chair of Urban Synergy, a mentoring charity, originating in Lewisham South East London, that one of our supporters and friends has provided such a timely and useful guide.

Courtenay Griffiths Q.C.

Prologue

All experiences provide the traveller with lessons. Whilst writing this book, I was taught a couple of important life lessons. Firstly, I am no writer. Writers are clearly extraordinary people. I say that because I found writing this book so very difficult. Secondly, I was reminded of the value of deadlines. Friend and foe alike will know how long ago I began this project, but it was not until I requested a deadline to ensure I meet a January 2017 publishing date that I actually got stuck in and covered more writing in 6 weeks than I had covered in the previous 6 years. Yes...six years.

But here it is. This is not a traditionally long worded book. I'm not like that. Even in my public speaking, I believe less is more. Only speak for as long as is absolutely necessary to get your point over.

Raising my son has been the greatest privilege of my adult life but I refused to write this book until I felt I could safely state that if he goes wrong now......it's his fault. LOL. I've laid down the basic programming. He's old enough to see and understand the example I have set for him. I am confident that he will do just fine in a world where he's going to need all the lessons I have taught him, plus many more which life will teach him.

What you will read in the next few pages is not the sum totally of my parenting experience, but just the key themes that I have used to guide my son. Some lessons were spoken, others via example, but all were of equal importance. Critically, I did not set out to create a mini me and if current results are to go by, I have not. He's nowhere near as handsome as I am and somehow he is taller............Kaream is his own man and that, if anything, was my plan all along.

To use the words of my long-time friend and poet Yasus Afari, this book is dedicated to my mother who fathered me. Not because my father was absent, but because that's what mothers did in those days.

Sleep well Carmel and I hope reading this book will raise a smile.

Chapter 1.

LOVE

1

Love thy self.

Everything begins with self-love. I want my son to appreciate who he is and never feel less than another person. Good solid self-esteem is one of the most important tools a young man needs to navigate this world. I believe that if you cannot love yourself, chances are you can never really love anyone else.

2

Love thy neighbour.

Your neighbour is far more than just the person next door. It is the lady on the bus, the man in the shop and yes, that youth by the chicken shop. If you begin each encounter from a position of love, then you are well on your way to creating a better world for all those you encounter and of course for yourself. No; there is no guarantee others will do the same, but it is better to extend an open palm than a fist.

3

Read *The Five Love Languages* by Dr. Gary Chapman.

Few books have had such an impact on my life. Finding *The Five Love Languages,* was like finding the Holy Grail of relationships and I am not prone to such exaggerations. Its beauty lies in the simplicity of its premise and the totally practical implications. This is as close as I have come to understanding women in all my years of having relationships with them.

4

One day someone will walk into your life and you will finally understand why it never worked out with anyone else.

We all have failures in intimate relationships, but never kick yourself too much when a relationship fails; adopt the principle that the next person will be 'the' person. Love and life are constant learning experiences. When something happens, just remember everything happens for a reason and you have some control over what that reason is. How? Well by opening your mind to the learning of every life event, good or bad. Romantic relationships require skill, so consider each one a class.

Chapter 2.
PEOPLE

5

Assume no one is stupid... until it's proven.

Two huge mistakes you can make are:

1. Underestimate others. Never under-estimate the other person. If you do, you leave yourself open to nasty surprises, and you may even place yourself at a disadvantage because of apathy.

2. Never be surprised when it is proven that someone is in fact, stupid; often only stupidity can explain some actions.

6

Never let others determine your course.

This is your life and this life is not a dress rehearsal. In the end, you will have only yourself to answer to about how your life turns out so don't rely upon or allow others to determine your outcomes. No one can make you do anything. In the end, your actions are your choices.....and you always have a choice.

7

Volunteer in your community.

When you volunteer, you have a great opportunity to learn new transferable skills, gain valuable experience and meet people from a variety of backgrounds. You will also gain the respect of your community and those who can change things in your life and in your community.

8

Show respect to your elders and learn from them.

Irrespective of academic achievements or money, your elders have experienced so much more than you. I suggest you take time out to learn from them. No, I am not suggesting you simply do the same things they did, or merely take their advice as gospel.

By talking to your elders, you can learn what things they did right and what things they did wrong. Avoid the wrong and copy the right. Call it a life cheat.

9

The blind cannot be forced to see.

Some people are "blinded" by their experiences and circumstances. You cannot force such a person to "see" your viewpoint no matter how logical. If the person is to be enlightened, the most you can do is provide new experiences and perhaps even a new environment and allow their eyes to open by themselves.

10

Scammers.

Times are hard. Those three words have meant that many will choose to cheat others. The modern polite word for cheats and thieves is 'scammer.'

Scammers play on your fears, desires and ego. Control all three. Remember this basic rule. If it appears to be too good to be true, chances are it is.

11

Different, but equal.

I have never understood the view that there should not be gender roles. I firmly believe in gender roles. Why? Because men and women are different. That difference is clearly reflected in our design so suggesting otherwise just makes no sense to me. On the other hand, we must be very careful not to confuse difference and different roles, with inequality.

Inequality stems from this traditionally male dominated society where women and their contributions are not valued as equal to that of men. In my view, the role of men and women should be complementary.

12

Egotism is the anesthetic that dulls the pain of stupidity.

Having an inflated view of one's self allows stupid people to sidestep their lack of intelligence and happily convince themselves and even others that all is well. But never forget that this is nothing but an illusion.

Chapter 3.
TIME

13

Be punctual.

Punctuality is a firm matter of respect. Whether it's the event organiser or other attendees turning up late for an event, it shows massive disrespect.

14

Time wasted, can never be regained.

You can never regain lost time, yes you can make up for past mistakes, but just imagine how much further ahead you would be today, had you done that which you should have done yesterday.

15

Always arrive very early for flights.

I guess if you have adopted point 10, be punctual, you will arrive early for all things, but arriving early for a flight has an extra bonus. Most free upgrades are given in the first 30 minutes of flight check-in.

Chapter 4.
RACE

16

Race does matter.

In a perfect world, the colour of your skin would not matter; but we don't live in a perfect world. We live in a world where people form and maintain stereotypical viewpoints of other people based purely upon skin colour. Remember racism is not just about thinking another race to be inferior, but it is also thinking your race is superior.

17

Just because they look like you, does not mean they are like you!

Skin colour does not signal sameness. Culture holds far better possibilities of sameness, than does skin colour.

18

Black Lives Matter.

This has become a divisive term, but I don't see why. Saying black lives matter should be a statement of fact for all people, irrespective of their race. Saying black lives matter does not in any way take away or diminish the importance of the lives of other races, however, it is a clear acknowledgement that for centuries black lives have appeared to be of a lesser importance than the lives of others. That cannot be disputed by any rational thinking human. The single greatest crime against humanity was without a doubt, the transatlantic slave trade......but no major information source will tell you this. Further blacks are consistently told to "get over" slavery while other races and groups are expected and saluted for their constant memorials to their dead. In short, we are being told black lives do not matter and that in their eyes they never have. This, my son, explains why anyone would consider such a sensible self-obvious statement, offensive and even aggressive.

19

There is no point complaining about racism, complaining about governments, complaining about employers or the lack of...and yet when asked we have no plan.

We, the people, need to uplift ourselves. Too many of us seem to still be waiting on the white man to stop being racist, on governments to take race laws seriously or on employers to stop discriminating. Meanwhile, we are like twigs on a river of racism, just along for the ride. We need our own plan, if not to end racism, but to survive and thrive in spite of it. Remember what happened when slaves were "given freedom?" They went right back into servitude because we had no plan. We were not organized. Here we are centuries later and still no plan.

Chapter 5.

HABITS & HOBBIES

20

Read.

When I was in high school, my Literature teacher encouraged me to read and to read widely. At the time, I thought she was just being a teacher. I now know that she was opening me up to a magical world. Books give not just information, but also are a cheap way to travel and see the world. To learn about diverse cultures and people you will never meet. I encourage you to read everything.

21

Take time out to listen and read the news.

You need to be informed way beyond your postcode. You are growing up in the first generation for which the world is truly your oyster. The news, though tainted with political, religious and moral bias, remains the best way to hear about and collect contrasting views about places you may never get the chance to visit.

22

Travel.

Develop the habit of travel. Nothing feeds the soul more than travel. When you travel, you will begin to understand your place in the world; how your people have contributed to this world and the value of other people.

23

Master technology.

Technology must become a tool for you. Your life will be dominated by technology which when you were born were just flights of fancy. To be left behind in technology is to be left behind in life. Make no one tell you otherwise.

24

Have fun.

Please have fun. Never allow the day-to-day of life to grind you down so much so that you forget to just have fun. Every now and then, indulge your inner child. This will keep you young.

25

It's OK to be untidy, but never be nasty.

Considering who I am, I could never tell you to be tidy, but I can tell you to never be nasty and, yes, there is a massive difference. Tidy, you can fix in a couple of minutes before the girlfriend pops around. Nasty means you need weeks to prepare and two deep cleans.

26

Own a good camera. Bad photos suck.

One of the other great inventions of this current era is the digital camera. Forget your phone and buy a great camera. Take lots of pictures and store them safely. Pictures connect your past to your present and can bring back the greatest of memories. Don't spoil your memories with a crap camera!!

27

Finish what you begin.

Stuff like this will define you as a real man or not. See things through because chances are you began them with a valid reasoning mind, so attaining that outcome should be a priority. Please don't think this means you cannot change your mind. Changing your mind is totally acceptable, giving up is not.

As you get older you will have children of your own and they will look to you for example, do not let my grandkids develop a defeatist or non-finisher attitude Always lead from the front.

28

Do the things you love.

When you are doing something you love, it's easy to get good at it and when you are good at something you love, you can change the world.

29

Your beliefs are not as important as your behaviours.

What you believe is internal; how you behave is external. Understand the difference, and you will understand that you can hold beliefs but never act on them unless you deem it totally necessary.

Chapter 6.

MONEY

30

Remember to learn about money.

This is one lesson I had to learn the hard way. Irrespective of all the academic accolades I achieved in early life, I did not learn anything about money and boy do I regret that. Understanding money, how it was created, how it works and, most importantly, how to make loads of it, is vital. Never let anyone convince you that money is the root of all evil. In my experience it is the lack of money that is the root of all evil. Almost every financial error I have made, I did so when I had the least money.

31

If you buy cheap, you buy twice.

I have had the privilege of spending time with some really great women. One such woman used to always say, "If you buy cheap, you buy twice" and, needless to say, she was so right. But this idea extends beyond just material things. If you buy into cheap ideas or beliefs you will find yourself constantly switching to different ideas and beliefs.

Be prepared to make huge investments to gain things of true value. And remember not all investments take the form of money!!

32

Money is not everything...... but it's bloody close.

Money is a strange thing. It can't make you happy, but without it life sucks. I guess it all comes down to how you choose to use your money. Some people will be happy with £40k per year while others are unhappy with £400k per year. Focus less on how much you earn and more on how to be happy with what you earn.

33

Humans must not be gifted with important things, but must work for them to fully realize the value of them.

This I learnt from your granddad. To value something, it must be given value. It takes a special type of person to understand the value of something which they have not worked for.

Chapter 7.
GOALS

34

Set goals.

This may sound very simplistic but many people fail in life, not through lack of ability or opportunity, but simply because they have no goals. Goals must be designed to stretch you and to give you a sense of satisfaction when achieved. The desire for that feeling of satisfaction will be your motivator. Remember that old saying "if you reach for the stars you may catch the moon" Set lofty goals!!!

35

Never be afraid to change direction.

Most people get lost because they fail to turn back at the first moment they become aware that they are off course, others because they are afraid to accept that they have taken the wrong road. If you have done everything in your power to pursue a single outcome and failed, don't simply keep repeating the process, change course. Do something different. Come at the problem from a different direction. Get a second opinion. Walk away, chill and come back with a fresh mind.

36

Stay away from the dream crushers.

Yes, you need a variety of people in your life, but make sure they are all facing the same way. Unfortunately, there are some people who are negative about all things or simply don't know how to support others. Spend as little time as possible with such people. Seek out those that will encourage and support your dream, those that find cheer in your success and make sure you do the same for them. Remember the universe tends to give you back whatever you put out.

37

"We must walk consciously only part way toward our goals and then leap in the dark to our success."
~ Henry David Thoreau

Getting to where you want to be cannot be planned for 100%, you must learn to take risks. These risks are reduced via preparation and experience. Remember ready, shoot, aim...

38

Stop thinking *"if only"*. Start thinking *"what now"*.

"If only..?" is all about dwelling in the past. And the answer to that question will never be one that changes the past. "What now..?" on the other hand, invokes that side of your mind which is designed to create solutions, generate ideas and make choices. Truth is, the longer you sit around thinking "if only..?" the more opportunities to correct mistakes of the past are slipping away. You can't change the past, no matter now often or how long you ask, "if only..?"

Remember, our lives are like books and each day is a page. We can't erase what has already been written but we can make the next page better.

39

"Nobody trips over mountains. It is the small pebble that causes you to stumble. Pass all the pebbles in your path and you will find you have crossed the mountain."

~Author Unknown

We can always see and act to avoid the big things in life, but the little things can and often do just slip by until it's too late. Don't ignore detail and remember that little things tend to add up if ignored.

Tony Robbins speaks about "chunking." This is the process of breaking huge tasks down into smaller parts. Think of these parts as life's pebbles. Deal with them one at a time rather than focusing on the problem or issue as one huge mountain.

40

**No matter how intelligent you are,
no matter how hard you work,
no matter how much you desire it...
you cannot fit a square peg into
a round hole...
at best there will be gaps.**

Some things just do not fit. Spend your time on the things that do fit. Put hard work and effort into the things that fit and your reward will be great. Trying to draw blood out of stone may sound noble, but is ultimately a waste of time.

41

The basics of a decent plan are what you want, by when, by who and the cost.

The project manager in me has tried to instill in you at least basic planning skills. No plan is complete without knowing what success looks like, when you want it by, who you need to execute it and, of course, what the cost is. Without these basic things, you don't have a plan; you have a wish or a dream but definitely not a plan. Having a life plan is not optional. Wealth or even just basic security for your children will depend on you having a plan in place. Watch out for those who try to entice you with words like, "freedom" when they don't know how to get to freedom.

PS. Not every plan must be detailed, but even a high-level plan is enough to get you going.

Chapter 8.

WOMEN

(Yeah they get their own section)

42

Women will be your greatest source of pleasure and pain.

Very little guidance I can give you on this one. Just enjoy the good times and endure the bad. Sometimes it will not feel like it, but they are well worth it!!

43

The love of a woman is transformational.

There are many signs of true love. However, perhaps the most overlooked is the transformation of your life, which will take place when a woman loves you and you love that woman back. It's been my experience that you will see things very differently once you are immersed in a loving relationship. Your very thought processes, decision-making processes, your tolerances ...all these will change.

44

Learn how to make your date feel like she is the only person in a crowded room.

To do this, you must make her feel special in the presence of other beautiful women. She must accidentally catch you admiring her. You must compliment her the moment that unbelievably stunning woman grabs everyone else's attention. Put that phone away....hell turn it off!

45

Winning a good woman's heart is actually very simple.

Here is how you do it. Dump all of your emotional baggage. Accept all of her emotional baggage. Don't be overly friendly with her female friends but befriend them all, especially the two who think you are up to no good and are only after sex. Accept all her male friends and dump all your female friends.

Never talk about your ex, but be understanding when she talks about her ex. Never spend more time in the mirror than her, but always look immaculate. Never forget important dates. Speak well, but let her speak. Compliment her regularly, but don't flatter her. Learn the difference between man shopping and woman shopping and accept that you will have to do some woman shopping.

Cook for her.

Never keep her waiting but never question her when she is late because you should know she was only late as she was making sure she was beautiful for you. Never fall into the, "how does this look on me?" trap. There is only ever one answer, "babe you make anything look great." Never, never be tempted to "keep it real" about how she is dressed...life is too short.

Always wear that scarf she bought for you (yes even if you hate it...it will grow on you). Leave her love notes where you know she will find them. Say nice things about her even when she thinks you think she can't hear them. Open doors for her. Be a MAN, be her MAN.

Oh sorry, I did say this was simple. Scrap all of that and just be yourself......

46

Men haters and feminist are two very different people.

Never get the two confused. A feminist pro-actively promotes equality for women and may even promote female superiority in a few areas. But she does not do so to deflate men.

A man hater simply hates all men. Why? Well, there can be a number of reasons, but suffice to say no man is ever going to be good enough or worthy. She is best left alone.

47

A woman will always forgive you for wanting to kiss her, but never for not wanting to.

As you will have gathered by now, delightful though they are, women are strange creatures. Believe me, a woman who does not want a kiss from you, will forgive you for attempting, but a woman who does want a kiss, will be deeply hurt that you did not even try!!

48

No woman is perfect, but there may just be a woman who is perfect for you.

When it comes to romance, to love and to partnership, remember this one: perfection is subjective. The ideal woman for you may not fit anyone else's idea of perfection, but that does not matter. Set realistic standards and when you see her, grab her. Her so-called imperfections may just be the opinions of others and you know what they say about opinions.

Chapter 9.

PERSONAL DEVELOPMENT

49

"Celebrate any progress, don't wait to get perfect."
~ Ann McGee Cooper

So much about your life will depend upon your ability to motivate yourself. One of the key ways to motivate other people is by giving praise, not flattery, but praise.

Waiting until a project or process is complete to celebrate, could leave you waiting for months, maybe even years to hear a 'well done' and even then you may still not hear it from an external source. Learn how to be you own personal cheerleader, but be honest. Only congratulate real milestones.

50

"Plan for the future, because it's where you are going to spend the rest of your life."
~ Mark Twain

Your life is not an accident and you can have a decent level of control over what happens in your life and thus the quality of your life. BUT you need a plan. This is not to say things will always go the way you plan, but just remember that a great plan comes with "what ifs". Not having a life plan is like going on the most important journey of your life, to a place you have never been, with no Sat Nav or even an A-Z! (Yeah I'm old school).

51

***"Being miserable is a habit;
being happy is a habit;
and the choice is yours."***
~ Tom Hopkins

It's been said that as humans we cannot always control the things that will and do happen to us. However, we can choose how we respond or react. Being miserable is a choice. Sure there will be times when it is the only real choice, but check yourself. Check yourself and I'm sure you will find times when you could make other choices, 'happiness' for example. Learn to change the context of events and you may just be able to find happiness in so much more.

52

"Vision is the art of seeing the invisible."
~ Jonathan Swift

Vision is akin to time travel. To have vision means you can see beyond that which already exist. Some much in life is invisible to most people, but those who have vision can see chances, value, beauty and much more in everything around them. Clearly, the fulfillment of vision comes with action.

53

Understand the power of compound interest.

When most people think of the term *compound interest* they think of money, bank rates and that sort of thing. Simply put, compound interest is the rate of interest applied to a total plus the interest and the rate applied again and again to the growing total or *principal* as it's called in financial circles.

In personal development circles, the application is different but the results can be astounding. If you could improve by just 1% each time you practiced a skill, you'd be over 100 times better than when you began with just 50 practice sessions. That, my son, is the power of compound interest and why practicing is so important.

54

"Continuous effort, not maximum strength or superior IQ, is the key to unlocking your potential as an achiever."
~ Greg Warner

No matter how strong or intelligent you may be, never doubt that there is someone else out there just as strong and as intelligent. However, to be the best, you also need continuous effort. It's that effort which converts potential into tangible success.

55

The meeting of preparation with opportunity generates the offspring we call luck.

Pure luck does not exist; never let people call you 'lucky'. No matter how 'lucky' someone is, in the end their preparation for that moment of opportunity is what will decide the ultimate outcome. Also remember that many people turn their backs on opportunities and never give themselves the chance to get 'lucky'.

56

Learn great communication skills.

Life is generally a series of relationships. You begin with the relationship with your family then you move on to relationships with your friends. Then colleagues at work, partners, business associates, your children and so on. The common theme underpinning all these relationships is communication.

A great communicator understands that communication is a two-way thing. It's not just about what you say or how you say it. It is also about how and whether you are able to listen. If you do not listen, chances are your responses will not match what is been said by the other person.

Remember, we communicate to convey ideas, thoughts and feelings and words are not the only way to do this, in fact, it's been proven that words are not even the most efficient way of getting your message across. Body language is oh so critical and again, remember, this works both ways. Learn not only to communicate using your body language but learn to read the body language of others. And a quick word of caution; once you understand that body language speaks loudly; remember that other people are watching your body language.

As a young black man, some will misunderstand your body language. Why? Fear, prejudice, social conditioning take your choice. Irrespective of this you still must learn how to communicate which such people. I'd suggest slow even tones, solid eye contact and limited hand gestures. Now for some this may sound like I'm asking you to be sheepish, I don't care, I just want you to get home each night.

57

In any presentation, discussion, debate or argument, it is essential that you know your audience.

Different audiences have different needs in order to 'hear' the same message. You may think your argument or viewpoint is rational and clear, but it's Chinese to the listener. So ask yourself....do your words and actions match the needs of the listener? Be aware of your environment. Remember Lesson 79.

This brings us to the question, "Who should adapt to ensure understanding?" Should the speaker adapt to the listener or should the listener adapt to the speaker?

I think the person sending the message should do everything in their power to adapt to the listener. After all, you are the one wishing to convey the message, right?

By the way, this is the basic premise of *The Five Love Languages* mentioned in Lesson 3.

Chapter 10.
WORK

58

If you can't get a job, make one.

Considering the way things are going in the world, this is perhaps the best piece of advice I have. There is nothing wrong with working for others, but it is not the only way. Creating your own job is extremely fulfilling and it can be highly lucrative. You become the manager of your time and your effort. You get to directly benefit from your efforts and feel the joy of success. That said, remember that self-employment is a double edged sword. You will have nowhere to hide from failure.

59

If you work for yourself, really work like you own the business.

As job finding has gotten harder the world has turned to self-employment. You can often see people proudly proclaiming themselves as business owners and typically they do so using fancy inflated titles ... *CEO* or *President*. What many do not readily tell us is that running your own business is hard...damn hard. No more paid sick leave, no more paid holiday leave, no guaranteed paycheck at the end of the month. No 'management' to blame for poor company strategy. As CEO you are not just the owner, but the accountant, the cleaner, the marketing dept., the mail room boy, head tea maker, sales manager and where the buck stops when the proverbial hits the fan.

However, the rewards for getting self-employment right are equally immense as long as you put in the work like your life depends on it, and it does. My advice so is to spend at least 18 months working for someone else to gain the skills, knowledge and attitudes required for your industry then make that leap and never look back. Oh and remember those transferable skills which you learnt helping that charity...

60

Find a career you love.

Growing up in Jamaica in the 70s and 80s, there used to be a Radio DJ named Barry G. Anyone who grew up in JA at that time knew how alive his broadcast would be. Great music was just a small part of his appeal. His energy and love for what he did came through with every word he spoke. He once explained it by saying this, "Management don't know, but they do not have to pay me to turn up and do my show every day. I love what I do and that's what people hear and feel when they listen to me." That's what you should aim for.

61

When you are doing something you love, it's easy to get good at it and when you are good at something you love, you can change the world.

When you have found that thing you love doing, you'll find it very easy to do it over and over. As I told you before, the more you practice or do something, the greater the chance that you'll get better at it.

When you combine great talent with a worthwhile job, it will not just change your life, it can change everything around you.

62

Never work hard, work smart.

Hard work is not just time consuming, it's often back breaking and with no assurance that the results will satisfy your needs. Try to work smart. Develop your working processes to improve your life while attaining the same, if not better, results. Remember, working is not the objective. The objective is the lifestyle which work affords you, so make sure you are able to enjoy that lifestyle. Too many people are too busy working hard, that they fail to enjoy life.

63

If you are going to be in business, be in business.

In the movie Brewsters Millions, actor Richard Pryor famously said, "We are in the business of doing business." Understand that Pryor's character was sent the task of WASTING US$1m. If you don't take your business seriously, you'll be doing the same, just with a lot less.

Having your own business is not just some nifty way of spending hours doing your own thing and not having to answer to anyone.... it's serious, business.

64

"The heights by great men reached and kept were not attained by sudden flight, but they, while their companions slept, were toiling upward in the night."

~ Henry Wadsworth Longfellow

People rarely know what it takes to be successful; too often they think success just sort of "happened." It does not (unless you are a reality TV star). You need to put in the work. Remember this, others may have the same ideas as you, at the same time as you, but you can beat them with your work rate.

Chapter 11.
LIFE

65

Play to win. No one remembers the guy who came second.

Usain Bolt made the 100m one of the most watched events over 3 consecutive Olympic Games. Millions watched his races, but few remember the guy(s) who came second in each of those three races. You must always plan to win, train to win, and play to win.

66

When you lose, don't lose the lesson.

If you've done your best and yet not achieved the best possible position, take time out to analyze the situation. What you are looking for are the clues as to why you did not achieve your goal. This is a vital action because many opportunities will actually come around again, maybe not in the same form, but if you learn the lessons of one failure, chances are you can use that information in another circumstance.

67

"Never back your opponents into corners."
~ The Art of War

People tend to up their game when backed into a corner. When people feel they have nothing to lose, that defeat is almost certain, they can be at their most dangerous.

68

Do not fear failure.

I could spend hours talking to you about this word, 'failure'. I've certainly done it enough but instead I'll like to suggest you see this word as having a very different meaning from that which you will find in the dictionary.

I'd like you to see the word failure as meaning lessons yet learnt. Why? Because that's all failure really is. When things don't go your way it is the best time to learn. Don't sulk, look into just went wrong. Be honest with yourself; what could you have done better or differently? What factors did you overlook? Speak to others and seek their help....then do it again. Once you have learnt all the lessons, you will find success. Remember, Success is merely a collection of learnt lessons.

69

Choices + actions = results.

Look past the waffle and life comes down to two things, the choices we make and the actions we take. First, you must make a choice. We always have choices, even when one choice is very, very difficult; it's still a choice. Having made the choice, you must then take action.

So you made your choice...but now you either act or not. Here's the thing, in life even doing nothing remains an action and so you must deal with the results. I'd like to suggest that you take positive action, rather than do nothing. Only by taking action can you help to guide your choices to a positive return.

70

"Ready, Fire, Aim." ~ Tony Robbins

I so wish this little nugget was mine, but it's not. Some people look at Ready, fire, aim and think it's a formula for disaster. But if you take a closer look it will really make sense. New recruits to the military are taught how to shoot using this exact method. Once they are ready they are told simply to fire the weapon, then they are told where the first shot hit. Then they are instructed to aim based upon that first shot.

In other words, sometimes you simply need to act, then assess and then act again, but this time you act based on the lessons learnt from your first action. Too often people sit waiting (aiming) for that perfect moment, they wait so long that often the moment passes. Take your best shot, self-analyze and shoot again, you'll be surprised at the outcome.

71

In life, where you are going is far more important than where you are coming from.

My driving instructor Mr. Louns, of the then Jamaica Telephone Company, used to tell us to focus 95% of our attention on where we were going. Pretty sound advice when driving and not too shabby in life. You cannot focus on that which is already gone and certainly not at the expense of what is to come. Keep your eyes firmly on your destination, as that will allow you to make the required adjustments to hit your target. The past is only there to learn lessons from......not to focus on.

72

Just because a lesson was taught, does not mean a lesson was learnt.

Don't ever think people will accept your opinion or even facts, just because you have carefully and eloquently made your case. The decision to learn, to accept, to grow is a conscious decision which people must make for themselves.

73

Every drop wears away the stone.

Jamaicans say "One one coco full basket." Scots say "every mickle makes a muckle." Life is not just about the big events. Even the small, hard to notice events all contribute to a much larger final outcome. As such it is not always necessary to wait until you can do the huge gestures, stay consistent with the small stuff....the result will be the same.

74

"It is easier to build strong children than to repair broken men."
~ Frederick Douglass

The older we get, the more entrenched our behaviours and habits become, so it's best to raise 'men' the way you'd like them to turn out. Too many parents consider issues of discipline as too harsh for young children. As a result, there are children who never really face constraints and rules until they have already formed poor behaviours. These poor behaviours are then hard to reverse.

In short, if you wish to 'train' a tree you should bend it when it is young.

75

Eat good food.

Note, I did not say healthy food. Son, eat stuff you like, do stuff you like. Enjoy your life because this is no dress rehearsal, this is it, and it will never get any more real than this. You must learn to live a life with no regrets. Good food is the second greatest pleasure you will encounter in this life.

76

Exercise – walk.

If you are going to eat what you want, you are going to need to exercise. Consistent walking is an effective way to get exercise. It's cheap and it's relatively low impact so the risk of injury is limited. Just make sure you invest in a decent pair of walking shoes and never forget some nice tunes to accompany you.

Not everyone loves the gym, so find a sport you love and play it. Join a local team and never give it up. Sure, as you get older, work and family will try to take over your time-don't let them. Blend your sport into your day to day life and you will reap huge rewards in fitness.

77

Invest in a great bed.

If you are going to spend big money on just one item of furniture, make it your bed. A great night's sleep is a basic requirement. Sleeping is when you recharge your body. But not all sleeps are equal. You can easily spend hours in a poor bed and wake up just as tired. Remember, beds are graded differently and should match your body type. I know it looks strange but go into the bed store and test out different beds before you buy....it will make such a difference.

Oh...never buy a bed smaller than a queen size. All the ladies in your life will thank me for this little nugget.

78

Only have a few friends, think quality not quantity.

When it comes to friends, the term "the more the merrier" does not apply. Friends are like diamonds, rare and precious. Great friendships must be cultivated and cared for. They take time to develop the strong connections that differentiate them from mere acquaintances.

Though finding great friends is difficult, the search is well worth it. They will endure any test and be there for you under all circumstances. They'll tell you when you are wrong and support you when you are right.

79

Become a mentor.

It's very difficult to mentor others without learning a vast amount about not just your mentee, but also yourself and even the world. Mentoring is about listening to another person, developing empathy for that person and their situation and then helping to guide them through a specific phase of their life.

To get mentoring right, you'll need to take many a step in your mentee's shoes. Such a journey forces you to view your own life very differently. Often we have no idea how good we have things or how to deal with things until we have the lives of others to compare ours to.

Another huge benefit of mentoring is this: sometimes we can offer great solutions to issues for others and it suddenly dawns on us that we could, and should, employ the same solutions within our lives. As they say, 'the best way to learn is to teach'.

80

Get a coach or a mentor.

The practice of Mentoring is as old as the hills. Literally meaning "wise advisor," Mentor is the name of the mythical Greek figure tasked by Odysseus to look after his son, Telemachus in his absence. I don't need to tell you the value of having a "wise advisor". Just imagine all the mistakes you could simply avoid but still have the benefit of the lessons such experiences would teach. A mentor can do that for you.

On the other hand, Coaching is a much more recent practice or so it appears. The word 'coaching' was used as far back as the 1830s, but coaching, as we know it, stems from the much more recent practice of Human Resource Development.

In fact, many of the first coaches that I came across were previously Human Resource Managers looking to change profession while going independent. Though much more costly then mentoring, coaching has a few clear advantages. The cost demands dedication from you. The intervention is short but fully immersive. Proper coaches never tell you what to do but via structured questioning, draw out your own expertise to provide the solutions for your issues. Their experience comes from understanding people. Their success comes from keeping you accountable.

81

Dress to suit your own sense of fashion. Just remember that every environment has its own uniform. Often, to get in, you must fit in.

This little piece of advice can on the surface appear to be contradictory, it's not. Maybe it should be two different lessons, but there's a point I need to make so here it is.

I need you to be your own man and since clothes maketh the man, you must never dress purely to follow fashion. Feel free to define for yourself what looks good on you.

That said, you also need to remember that life is all about uniforms and uniforms serve a purpose. You are allowed to have more than one uniform, one to suit each environment in which you wish to operate.

82

Truth is constant and has no expiration date.

In this age of social media, it can seem like the Truth is subjective, changeable, often even based on opinion and what's currently in fashion. I need you to understand that the truth never changes, your perception may, but it does not. Don't get caught up in senseless debates with people who use phrases like, "my truth" or even worse, "my opinion". They are deflecting because they cannot prove the things they say.

That said, do not assume that the things you believe to be true are automatically so. Check, read, speak to others. Use Vulcan-like logic to come to the truth and when you do, remember that you still do not have the right to force that truth onto others. We are all on the different journeys, but even those heading your way may be at different points in that journey. So sometimes you need to just let people realize truth for themselves...or not.

83

Awe and Envy are twins.

Yep, awe and envy can often look exactly the same but are very different characters, so take your time to decide which is actually in play. In the words of Ra's al Ghul "be aware of your surroundings", know who your supporters are and who your detractors are. Confusing the two is extremely dangerous.

84

Change your conversation & possibly your association – Your focus is your reality.

I promised not to be too deep in writing this book, but here is one example where a little depth is required. Son, you have the power to decide your reality and that power is wrapped up in how you choose to see the world. And yes I said choose.

A Jewish holocaust survivor attributed his survival to the fact that he told himself every day that the prison camp was instead a holiday home and the guards his servants. He painted himself such a vivid picture that nothing they did to him had a lasting effect. He chose his reality and you can too.

85

"When they go low, we go high." **~ Michelle Obama**

Never sink to the low depths of an enemy, remember the gutter is their natural habitat so they will beat you on experience if you join them there. Maintain your dignity, show class and poise no matter what they do.

86

"Boat don't sink until the water comes in."
~ Diana Mckensie

No matter how tatty a boat may be, it will not sink until water comes in. You may be down, but until you are knocked out....you still have a chance.

Defeat in so many situations is a state of mind. Giving up before the fat lady has sung results in only one sure thing...you lose. Fight to the end. Never give up never surrender.

87

Politeness has become so rare that some people mistake it for flirtation.

When I was growing up in Jamaica, you could never pass someone without a greeting of some kind. Men were still being taught to open doors for women. Children to say 'please' and 'thank you'. Yet, somehow, this current generation of adults are so impolite that people are suspicious of your intent if you are polite. Oh....I also blame feminism or should I say some women's interpretation of feminism. Opening a door for a woman is now almost a capital crime. (My editor is screaming "not true".)

88

**Every day bucket go ah well,
one day di bottom a go fall out.**

Son, you can't keep adding stress or using something and expect it to last forever. Nothing does. Be aware of the stress you may be causing others and be ready to offer a healing hand to those who work for and with you to help refresh them for the next round of work.

89

All actions have consequences and you don't get to decide what the consequences are.

Think about this before you act because once you do, you become liable for the consequences of your actions. Consequences are a must. You can't outrun them and when they hit, you'll find you have no power over what those consequences are.

90

Just because I can do it on my own, does not mean I want to.

Whether you believe in God or nature, the fact is God/Nature thought it would be a great idea to design life on the basic principle of Two. Furthermore, everything on earth depends on other things, so why should you opt to 'go it alone?'

I do hope you are self-sufficient but not so much so that you don't see the need and value of working with others. Learn to share tasks and successes. Rest assured they will feel so much better when the whole experience is shared.

91

Wi cum fi drink milk nuh fi count cow!!!!

This lesson is based on one of my favorite Jamaican sayings. Why is it one of my favorites? Well, I just love the confusion it causes among my UK friends, black and white alike. They just don't get it. Son, never be tempted to just turn up or to 'just take part.' When you enter anything, it must be to win. Let someone else count the cows. You, my son, are here for one reason and one reason alone, to reap the benefits of the situation. Brits, will not like this. Hell, they still celebrate when their athletes come 2nd in the heats but for you, my son, you need to understand that second place is not good enough. Never was and never will be.

HOWEVER this does not mean no one else must be allowed to drink milk, normally there is more than enough milk to go around. But remember we are not spectators.

Chapter 12.
EDUCATION

92

School is easy. All you have to do is turn up, sit down and shut up.

Perhaps the simplest part of your life will be your school days. Nothing complex is requested of you. I'll deal with the hard stuff on your behalf.

School is where you will begin to learn not just the academics that you will need, but also the social skills. Unfortunately too many youngsters (and their parents) don't understand the student's role during their time in school. Put simply, your role in school is to be a sponge. Absorb everything around you. Then the role of your parents is to provide context for the skills you learn and to help you shape those lessons into attitudes, habits and behaviours. The problem is humans are not that great at multitasking, so if you are talking while you should be listening, chances are the lessons taught will not be learnt. So just shut up and listen. Oh...and turning up is pretty useful too. LOL!

93

No, I did not send you to school to like the teacher. If you do, that is a pleasant bonus.

This is one of the greatest misunderstandings you will encounter in your school life. I don't need you to like your teacher. It's not a requirement. I expect you to learn. Sure, that task would be easier if you did like the teacher, but liking someone or not must never be an excuse for underachievement. You see, you'll soon be out of school and into the workplace and rest assured that you have no guarantee that you will like your boss or colleagues. You have an even less guarantee that they will like you. Does this mean you'll never work?

Son, school, a good school, is designed to prepare you for the real world. Not liking someone is going to be the least of your issues in the real world. Put you big boy pants on and deal with it. Always think about your objective. See them merely as a means to an end.

94

"If you're not prepared to be wrong, you'll never come up with anything original."
~Ken Robinson

The fear of being wrong, like the fear of failure, can be debilitating. Accept that you will not always get things right, but that each failure brings you closer to that which is right. When asked about his 10,000 errors Thomas Edison reportedly quipped, "I have not failed. I have found 10,000 ways that do not work." Importantly, he carried on and 'invented' one of the world's greatest inventions.

95

Curiosity is the soil of knowledge.

Going to school is not the only way that you will gain knowledge. Human curiosity drives mankind to discover more and more about ourselves and all that surrounds us. Tap into your natural curiosity and never fear asking questions, doing research, reading and talking to people who have different experiences than you do. That curiosity will tap into much knowledge...

96

Never let anyone tell you there is no God.

I was never big on church or organized religion for that matter and I am not overly spiritual. However, I have a very strong belief in God. How could I not? I'd like you to strip away all that you have been told. Look around you and, as I did, come to the simple understanding that nothing you see around you is random. How could it be? Mankind is limited by the belief that if we can't do something, it cannot be done.

We are classic victims of our own arrogance. Those who think this is all just the result of chaos or evolution forget that something must have created that first big bang. They forget that chaos is gone and now order is in place...why? How? Be brave and not only ask yourself these important questions but keep an open mind to the possible answers. A closed mind will force you to accept the simple easy answers.

Chapter 13.
PARENTING

97

Develop strong communication links with your children early; you are going to need them later.

One of the tricks to parenting is great communications. But too often parents wait too long to develop communication links with their children. Begin day one. Yes, long before you are even convinced that they understand what you are saying. Remember communications is a two-way thing, so a huge part of developing great communication links is to ensure that your children feel that they can ALWAYS speak to you about anything. This does not mean they always will, but make sure it is at least an option. As children get older, they will begin receiving and soliciting advice from all quarters; make sure they see you as a safe port of call. Create environments where conversations are encouraged. Get a dining table, eat as a family and listen to your kids. Encourage them to speak about the trivial and that will help when something more important needs to be discussed.

98

As a parent be Consistent.

They say there is no parenting manual, so here is my best advice to you for when you become a parent, be consistent, children thrive on consistency. Even the most disciplined of environments are bearable if the child knows what to expect. Moving boundaries and changing rules only serves to confuse the child.

99

Same water soften potato.... harden egg!!!

By now you will have heard a parent say, "I don't know how 'he' turned out like that. Look at his brother? I treated them the same." LOL. Yeah, that's the issue. Humans are individual and as such you cannot reasonably expect two humans to behave or react the very same way to the same stimulus or environment. It will not work.

Take your time to evaluate people as individuals and don't be lazy. Treat people as you find them, not based on predetermined expectations.

100

One of the primary duties of any parent is to consistently beat your children at games. Once they get old enough to beat you or spot that you are cheating... you then show no interest.

LOL......Now you understand why you lost all those games we play together. I hope this is a lesson you have learnt and are now ready to use with your children when they come along. Trust me, you'll have hours of fun with this one. I know I did.

101

You may have been born in Lewisham but you are Jamaican. Understand what that means.

When watching sports, and by sport I mean Athletics, we cheer for Jamaica. Does not matter whether they are coming 1st or 8th. We cheer for Jamaica. No Jamaican in the race? Then we are cheering for anyone from an African or Caribbean country who appears to have even half a chance.

No Africans, Caribbean or Jamaicans in the race? Then all finalists must be on drugs and we don't cheer for drug cheats.

PS....We might cheer for Canadians. Yes, we like Canadians...they are so polite.

Chapter 14.

BRAWTA

102

When dealing with the police, your first duty is to just get home.

When you encounter a police officer and you will, your first and primary duty is to get home safely. I have witnessed too many young men who get this wrong and appear to believe that it is their duty is to appear funny for the benefit of their friends or to ridicule the officer again for the amusement of their friends.

I need you to enter into each such engagement with police officers with this lesson in mind. If you do you will tailor your responses to that end and your outcomes will be far less confrontational. Never forget you do not have the power of arrest over the officer, but he does have it over you.

103

Never judge a man by where he is, if you must, judge him by how he got there.

Try never to judge people. However, sometimes you may need to and if you do try first to understand their journey. It is their journey rather than their current status that will inform you as to the person in front of you.

About the Author

"101 Lessons I Taught My Son" is Paul's first book. The book reflects Paul's upbringing as a child in Jamaica but is compounded by the very different parenting culture in the UK where he has brought up his son Kaream.

Faced with raising a young black boy in the UK, Paul sought help and in the first instance, he found that support in The 100 Black Men of London, an international organisation dedicated to community development and particularly focused on young people. Paul served many roles in the 100, but importantly this was his first taste of mentoring and coaching of young people. Paul went on to develop a leading Mentor Training program which he has delivered to a variety of organisations across London.

Paul's Mentoring Training program brought him to the attention of Urban Synergy one of London premier mentoring organisations. Urban Synergy was eagerly seeking out a quality mentor training for their new recruits, and Paul's program was select. Ten years later Paul still trains All Urban Synergy Mentors and serves as a board trustee.

Paul holds a Masters in Project Management and works as a Consultant Program/Project Manager.